FIRST IMPRESSIONS

FIRST IMPRESSIONS

Paul Gauguin

HOWARD GREENFELD

Harry N. Abrams, Inc., Publishers

SERIES EDITOR: Robert Morton
EDITOR: Ellen Rosefsky
DESIGNER: Joan Lockhart
PHOTO RESEARCH: Colin Scott

LIBRARY OF CONGRESS CATALOGING-IN-PUBLICATION DATA

Greenfeld, Howard.
Paul Gauguin / Howard Greenfeld.
p. cm. — (First Impressions)
Summary: Examines the life and work of the nineteenth-century post-Impressionist
painter known for his use of bright colors and his depiction of
South Seas scenes.
ISBN 0–8109–3376–4
1. Gauguin, Paul, 1848–1903—Criticism and inter-
pretation—Juvenile literature. [1. Gauguin, Paul,
1848–1903. 2. Artists.] I. Title. II. Series.
ND553.G27G75   1993
759.4—dc20
[B]   93–9454
                              CIP
                              AC

Printed and bound in Hong Kong

Chapter One

The Early Years

Paul Gauguin was a successful stockbroker in Paris, who, at the age of thirty-five, made a dramatic decision to give up everything—his secure future, comfortable home, and loving family—in order to pursue a difficult career as a painter. He ended his life, twenty years later, living as an outsider in lonely exile among the primitive societies of the South seas.

His story is as exciting as it is colorful, but the truth is a little less exotic and dramatic. Gauguin was, without doubt, a courageous man, who relentlessly pursued his dream. Many considered him, primarily, a bold and daring genius who refused to compromise, a sensitive artist with a deep hatred of hypocrisy. For others, he was vain and arrogant, stubborn, sometimes violent, and totally insensitive to the needs of his family and friends.

In fact, he was all of these things, at different times. He was neither loveable nor likeable, but there is no reason why a great artist must be loveable or likeable. Nonetheless, his life was—even when the truth has been separated from the legend—a marvelous one. Not a child genius like Leonardo or Michelangelo or Picasso who showed extraordinary artistic ability when very young, Gauguin developed new and profound interests even when mature, and proved that it was possible, at any time, to change one's career and goals and way of life. In the case of Gauguin, this change resulted in the development of an innovative creative artist who gave everything to his art and whose paintings and ideas have had a significant influ-

Self-Portrait for Carrière. *1888/89*
This self-portrait of the artist shows him wearing the Breton vest
in which he was often photographed.

ence on the course of modern art.

Paul Gauguin's eccentricities, his passion for the exotic, and his stubbornness can be traced to his ancestors. Flora Tristan, his maternal grandmother, was an extraordinary woman. Born in 1803 of a French mother and a Peruvian father, she was a beautiful, passionate, and outspoken rebel who devoted her entire life to fighting for revolutionary causes. Her personal life, however, was tragic. Her marriage, at the age of seventeen, to a gifted painter-lithographer, André Chazal, was a failure. When Flora Tristan died, in 1844, she left her nineteen-year-old daughter, Aline, alone. Soon after her mother's death, Aline married Clovis Gauguin. Eleven years older than his bride, Clovis came from a comfortable family of shopkeepers in Orléans, a city in the heart of France. He had come to Paris in his early twenties to work as a political writer for *Le National*.

On April 29, 1847, their first child, Marie, was born. On June 7, 1848, Aline gave birth to their second child, a son. Christened Eugène Henri Paul Gauguin, he was to be simply known as Paul Gauguin. His birth took place during a time of ugly violence and bitter street fighting.

For Clovis Gauguin this turmoil had a personal meaning. Foreseeing a return to the monarchy he and his newspaper had vigorously opposed, he decided it would be best to emigrate to Lima, Peru, where he might be able to start a newspaper of his own with, he hoped, the help of his wife's influential and wealthy great-uncle.

The family left France for Peru on August 8, 1849. Their voyage ended in tragedy even before they reached their destination. On October 30, Clovis died of a ruptured blood vessel. Instead of arriving in Lima filled with expectations of a bright future, Aline arrived as a poor widow, alone in a strange land with two small children.

Aline need not have feared. Her mother's family welcomed her with warmth and generosity. During her five years in Peru, Aline was treated like the spoiled child of a large, wealthy family. She flourished and radiated a new-found charm and self-confidence. In fact, it was not as a drab, sweet housewife that Paul later remembered his mother in a portrait, but as a noble and graceful Spanish lady, dressed colorfully in the native costume of Peru; not merely gentle and pure, but quick tempered and fiery.

As for Paul, the years in Lima were remembered as an exotic fairy tale. They were a source of perpetual enchantment. His life in semitropical Peru, where it rarely rained but earthquakes were common, had a lasting effect on him as did his association with a wide variety of people he would never have known in France—Chinese, Indians, and blacks were a part of his daily life. He never forgot the sight of a young Chinese servant ironing his family's clothing, the grocery store where he would sit between two barrels of molasses sucking on sugar cane, and the playful monkeys, Peru's most common domestic animals. All of this left an indelible impression on the boy.

In 1855, however, this splendid period came to an end when Aline and her children returned to France at the request of her father-in-law, who was dying. Matters of his estate and the family's inheritance had to be settled. Even more important, as much as Aline enjoyed her sheltered life of luxury in Peru, she missed France and knew it was time for her children to begin school in their native country. Paul, seven years old at the time, didn't even know his native language and spoke only Spanish.

The return to France, to Orléans, where the family first lived in order to be near Paul's father's family, was difficult for the young boy. Life in the gray, gloomy city of Orléans was far different from the life he had led in the warm, lush tropics. In Lima he had been free to do as he pleased, while in Orléans he had to submit to discipline and attend school with the children of ordinary shopkeepers, boys and girls who shared neither his past experiences nor his dreams of an exotic future.

After a few years, unable to make a decent living in Orléans, Gauguin's mother moved to Paris, where she set up shop as a dressmaker. She had to leave Paul behind in a church-supported boarding school until she could take proper care of him in her new home.

Paul's schooling, in Orléans and in Paris, apparently made little impression on him. For the most part, he was a poor student, not because he lacked intelligence but because he was an arrogant youngster. He was so certain that he was better than all the other students that he never bothered to study. Socially, he was a failure, too. He was unable to make friends, since he did little to hide his opinion that most of his classmates were fools.

At the age of seventeen, Gauguin's formal education came to an end.

Though his grades had been poor, he had become an avid reader and a keen observer of the world around him. Arrogance, not ignorance, was his problem. At a time when young men his age were in school, finding jobs, and settling down, he had only one dream: to become a sailor. As a sailor he could perhaps rediscover the enchanted world in which he had been raised.

To begin, he enlisted as an officer's candidate in the merchant marine and, in December 1865, was assigned to a cargo ship bound from the port of Le Havre, France, to Rio de Janeiro, Brazil. This was the first of several voyages he took over the next few years; voyages, as he had hoped, to give him a chance to explore the world. Not surprisingly, he was most excited by the charms of the tropics, which had been such a great part of his childhood.

Soon young Gauguin learned that his childhood had come to an end. During a stopover in India, he received word that his mother, his only solid link to his early years, had died in St. Cloud, near Paris, on July 7, 1867. She was only forty years old. It was a tragedy that affected him deeply. In her will, he learned later, Aline indicated that she knew her son well, suggesting in her testament that he "get on his career, since he has made himself so dis-

Photos of Paul Gauguin (left) and Mette Sophie Gad (right) were taken in 1873, the year of their marriage. At that time, they seemed to be ideally suited to one another.

liked by all my friends that he will one day find himself alone." Gauguin, however, was not yet ready to get on with a serious career; there was more of the world to be seen. In January 1868, he left the merchant marine and enlisted in the navy. Two months later, he was assigned to service aboard the *Jérôme-Napoléon*, a 450-horsepower corvette.

For more than three years, the *Jérôme-Napoléon* cruised the Mediterranean, the Black Sea, and the North Sea, making stops at London, Naples, Corfu, the Dalmatian coast, Trieste, Venice, Bergen, and Copenhagen. Gauguin grew tired of his life in the navy; he hated its discipline and the roughness of his shipmates. In April 1871, he was discharged.

Though those final years at sea must have been unhappy ones, it was during that period Gauguin grew up physically and emotionally. Still as short as he had been throughout his childhood (he was barely five feet, four inches tall when he joined the navy), he had become a powerfully built, broad-shouldered young man who could, and often had to, hold his own in a fight. His life as a sailor had taught him to take care of himself and be more independent. In some ways, however, he had yet to mature. He was still unable to decide how to make use of his abilities, and still unable, at the age of twenty-three, to choose a career.

With this in mind, Gauguin traveled to St. Cloud immediately following his discharge. There he was astonished to learn that his mother's house had been burned down by the Prussians, then at war with the French, in 1870. With that fire, the young man had lost not only a home but also part of a legacy—paintings and valuable objects that his mother had collected in Peru. But his mother had left him a far more important legacy, a wise and cultured guardian, whose influence on Paul Gauguin would be invaluable.

That guardian, Gustave Arosa, was a wealthy businessman as well as a talented photographer and a patron of the arts. His large collection included several works by some of the finest painters of his time—Delacroix (who was a close friend of his), Corot, Courbet, Daumier, and several artists who would later become known as the Impressionists.

Arosa took the responsibility as Gauguin's guardian most seriously. As a first step, he found him a position in Paris working for a stockbroker, Paul Bertin. The job, acting as a middleman between stockbrokers and their clients, was a good one, and Gauguin, though he had had no experience or training in the field, soon became proficient at it. But he wasn't deeply satisfied by it. Nonetheless, he had in a surprisingly short time found a career that he could pursue. It was time to put other aspects of his life in order.

Life outside of his job was quiet. He was by nature a rather solitary man who, when the day's work was done, would usually return to his modest apartment where he would spend his evenings reading his favorite authors, Edgar Allan Poe and the French writers Charles Baudelaire and Honoré de Balzac. On Saturdays, however, he would go out, most often to a dance hall. He liked to dance, and he very much enjoyed the company of women.

It was a calm and pleasant life, far different from the life he had led during his years as a sailor. Yet it was in many ways a lonely life for Gauguin, who felt superior to his colleagues at the office as he had to his schoolmates and made few friends. Among these few, however, was a fellow employee, Emile Schuffenecker, who would play an important role in his life. Schuff, as he was known, was a good-natured man, three-and-a-half years younger than Gauguin. Schuff was merely a poorly paid clerk, whose future did not seem nearly so bright as Gauguin's did. What drew the two men together had nothing to do with their jobs; it was their common enthusiasm for drawing and painting, which for Schuff was already a serious hobby and had started to interest Gauguin through his friendship with Arosa.

Gauguin's position in the firm was an enviable one; his increasing enthusiasm for art proved to be a stimulating distraction, and his friendship with Schuff provided him with the male companionship he needed. Now he was ready to take on the responsibilities of a wife, a home, and a family.

In the autumn of 1872, Gauguin met a woman with whom to share his life. Her name was Mette Sophie Gad. Born on a small Danish island, Mette and her siblings were brought up in Copenhagen by their widowed mother. Even at an early age, Mette had shown signs of the independence and strength that would characterize her behavior all of her life. At the age of seventeen, she left home to take a position as governess to the children of the prime minister of Denmark. This enabled her to come into contact with a social and intellectual world she had never known in her conventional middle-class home. Through the people she met, her outlook broadened and her knowledge of the world beyond Denmark grew, so much so that, by the time she was twenty-two years old, she was ready to accept an offer by the wealthy father of one of her friends, Marie Heegaard, to join his daughter as a companion and guide on an extended visit to Paris.

It was during this visit to the French capital that Gauguin met the two Danish women. Though he was impressed by both of them, he was especially attracted to the vital young Mette who was so unlike the superficial French women he had known. Mette's keen intelligence and forthrightness set her apart from the others, as did her lack of pretensions.

In a very short time, their friendship grew. At first, Gauguin would meet both women for lunch, but soon he and Mette began to meet alone. Their talks became increasingly personal and intimate, and in January 1873, only a few months after their first meetings, they made plans to marry.

The wedding took place on November 22, 1873; the bride was twenty-three years old, and the groom twenty-five. They had the whole world before them, and they delighted at the prospect. As they set up their house in a comfortable apartment in Paris, their future seemed secure.

Chapter Two

A Momentous Decision

For the first few years, their marriage seemed an ideal one. In spite of the stock market crash in 1873 and a long period of unsettled economic conditions in France and much of Europe, the young stockbroker continued to prosper. Gauguin's investments had been sound ones, and he was able to provide more than adequately for his family. His family grew in number. Emile, a son, was born in 1874; a daughter, Aline, was born in 1877; a second son, Clovis, was born in 1879. It was, on the surface at least, the perfect household—a loving husband and wife, happy, healthy children, and, for the head of the family, the anticipation of a brilliant business career.

Nonetheless, during these first apparently tranquil years, a significant change was taking place, one that Mette failed to recognize at the time, but would deeply affect their lives. Even before the birth of their first child, Gauguin's interest in art was developing into a passion and was gradually beginning to dominate his thoughts.

His friendship with Schuff was partially responsible for this. At first, the two men merely talked about art, but soon Gauguin's colleague encouraged him to try a hand at painting. In the beginning, Gauguin was content to enjoy this as a hobby. Often on Sundays, usually in the company of Schuff, he would take his paint box and easel to the countryside outside Paris, and, on occasional evenings, he would join his friend at a nearby school for artists, the Académie Colarossi, where they would sketch and paint from models. Gradually, however, encouraged by those who had seen his work and had liked it, he began to take his own art more seriously and to devote more time to it. By 1876, he felt so sure of himself that he sent one of his landscape paintings to the Salon, the annual government-sponsored exhibition, where it was accepted by the jury and hung alongside the works of experienced professional painters. The mere acceptance by this jury was a surprise, since the Salon was by far the most important of all Parisian exhibitions. Even more astounding was the fact that Gauguin's painting was actually singled out by one critic as showing promise. The stockbroker who had never formally studied art had every reason to be proud of himself. Yet, for some reason, he told neither his wife nor his close friend Schuff of this success.

Gauguin's passion for painting increased, and an even more profound influence than Schuff was that of Gauguin's guardian, Gustave Arosa. Art was a topic for lively discussion and debate at Arosa's homes—in Paris and in St. Cloud—which Gauguin visited frequently. The paintings that hung on the walls of these homes stimulated him to visit museums and private art

The Impressionist painter Camille Pissarro was one of Gauguin's early mentors, who gave the younger artist his time and his knowledge generously. Pissarro added his sketch of Gauguin (left) to one of himself that Gauguin had presented to his mentor.

The Schuffenecker Family. *1889*

Gauguin was staying at the home of the Schuffeneckers when he painted this unflattering portrait of the family. Louise Schuffenecker, whom Gauguin had described as a "pest," looks bitter and sad, while there is something pathetic and servile about Schuff gazing at his wife.

galleries, where he sharpened his eye and developed a critical understanding of the forms and techniques of painting. He learned from and liked much of what he saw, but he was especially drawn to the paintings of a small band of courageous artists—Claude Monet, Pierre-Auguste Renoir, Alfred Sisley, and Camille Pissarro—who were to become known as the Impressionists.

The Impressionists had found a new method of artistic expression, developing what at that time was considered a startling new technique.

They used small brush strokes, dabs of rich pure color, to capture on canvas not a static scene but a fleeting impression. They worked in direct contact with nature, unlike other painters who, even if they began work outside, completed their canvases in their studios.

The results of their daring experiments were brilliant, yet their struggle to have their works shown to the public was a long and difficult one. The jury of the official Salon—the same one that accepted Gauguin's competent but unexceptional landscape—rejected the Impressionists' paintings as too revolutionary, and very few private galleries were willing to show them.

Gauguin, at the beginning of his development as a painter, was far from indifferent to these paintings. On the contrary, he was as excited by what he saw in the galleries, as he was by those in Arosa's home. He began to buy them, and by 1880 he had a collection of outstanding Impressionist works. Furthermore, he had a chance, through Arosa, to meet many of the artists, among them the man who would become his first mentor, Camille Pissarro.

Pissarro's background was as exotic as his own. Born in 1831 on the island of St. Thomas in the West Indies, he was the son of a Creole mother and a Portuguese-Jewish father. At the age of twelve, his parents sent him to Paris to be educated. It was there that he first developed an interest in art, and, in 1847, when he returned home to work in his father's general store, he spent more and more of his time sketching local scenes. His family was strongly opposed to his idea of becoming a professional painter, but the young man defied them. In 1852 he ran off to Venezuela to escape the dreary prospect of a future as a shopkeeper. A few years later, his family gave in to his wishes, giving him permission to return to Paris, where he could best pursue his career as an artist. There, after his work was rejected repeatedly by official circles, he joined forces with those painters who would lead the Impressionist revolution.

It was Pissarro who guided Gauguin as he developed from a very gifted amateur painter into a serious professional artist. During the summers of 1879, 1880, and 1881, the two men often painted together at Pontoise, a small village near Paris, where Pissarro and his family had lived since 1866. During these years, Pissarro taught Gauguin to change the colors of his palette, to concentrate on the three primary colors—red, blue, and yellow— and their complementaries—green, orange, and violet.

In addition to serving as Gauguin's teacher, Pissarro introduced the younger man to his circle of friends, among them the Impressionists. These men took Gauguin seriously as an artist, and soon he was invited to show his work at the exhibitions that they organized annually as a protest to the official Salon which had shunned them. In 1879, Gauguin entered a marble portrait head of his son Emile at the fourth Impressionist Exhibition. (He had learned the art of sculpture from a neighbor, a marble cutter.) The following year he showed another marble bust, this time of Mette, as well as several canvases—land- scapes and scenes of Pontoise, which he had painted the previous summer with Pissarro. Gauguin's work was noted by crit- ics of this last exhibition, as was his stylis- tic indebtedness to Pissarro.

Gauguin's participation in the sixth Impressionist Exhibition, which took place in April 1881, marked a turning point in his career. For the first time, he was praised by an in- fluential critic, J. K. Huysmans, a novelist and poet who was among the first critics to

Snow Scene. *1883*

Gauguin painted this large and ambitious painting while he was influenced by the Impressionists. It is believed to show the garden of a home Gauguin rented in Paris from 1880 to 1883.

appreciate the paintings of the Impressionists. Huysmans singled out a nude study which he felt revealed in Gauguin "a modern painter's temperament." He added: "among contemporary painters who have treated the nude, none has yet given so passionate an expression of reality."

Understandably, these words from a powerful critic were of great encouragement to Gauguin. Yet his doubts only increased the following year, when thirteen of his works shown at the seventh Impressionist Exhibition were coldly received, even by Huysmans.

Clearly, it was time to choose between his painting and his business career. This choice was made easier by an event beyond Gauguin's control. In January 1882, the stock market collapsed. Investors, large and small, lost their money, companies were forced into bankruptcy, and stockbrokers were fired. As a result, his job was in jeopardy. This seemed the right time to make a move. He decided to give up his job in business and devote all of his energy to painting, no matter what the consequences.

The news that her husband had left his job came as a shock to Mette. Of course, she had been aware of his increasing passion for art, but she had failed to recognize the depths of that passion. After all, he had a family to support, and to do that he would have to find another job so that they could continue to live in the comfortable manner to which she was accustomed.

Gauguin also worried. Another child was expected later that year, and he had to make a living. He turned to Pissarro for help. "I find myself now in inextricable difficulties," he wrote him. "I have a large family and a wife who is incapable of enduring misery. Thus I cannot devote myself entirely to painting without being assured of at least having half of the indispensable. . . . it is absolutely necessary that I find my livelihood with painting."

Pissarro was sympathetic, but he could offer no help. He had known what it was to struggle as an artist for many years, for he too had a large family he was barely able to support. But he worried that Gauguin was too concerned with making a living and too afraid of that struggle.

In this, Pissarro underestimated the determination of his friend. Gauguin had made up his mind: in his own eyes, he was already a painter. On the birth certificate of his fifth child, Pola, a son born on December 6, 1883, he listed his occupation as "artist-painter." There would be no turning back.

Chapter Three

Early Struggles

Gauguin's decision to devote his life to his art, whether it was courageous or irresponsible, brought about an enormous change in the everyday life of his family. Their savings had been depleted in the stock market crash, and their income was practically nonexistent. Mette was especially distressed; instead of being the wife of an affluent businessman, she would now have to adjust to being the wife of a struggling artist.

The first change in their way of life involved moving out of their elegant Parisian home, which they could obviously no longer afford. Instead of finding more modest quarters in the capital, Gauguin decided, in early 1884, to move his family to an apartment in the port city of Rouen in northern France, where living would cost less than it did in Paris. Pissarro had lived and painted there the previous year, apparently with considerable success, and Gauguin felt that his art, too, might flourish away from Paris. He wanted to develop his own style and not imitate the Impressionists. Besides, he was certain that he could sell his paintings to the citizens of Rouen and receive lucrative portrait commissions from them.

Rouen, however, proved to be a disappointment. Living there was not as inexpensive as Gauguin had expected, and the few residents who bought paintings showed little or no interest in his portraits or his landscapes. As an artist, in Rouen as in Paris, Gauguin found it extremely difficult to furnish his family with even the bare necessities. Mette suffered, too. Her husband, whose principles and goals now seemed so different from her own, was becoming a stranger to her.

The situation worsened steadily. By July, little more than six months after their arrival, they had become so desperate that Gauguin was forced to sell his insurance policy for half its value. And by early autumn, Mette

was able to convince him that only a move to Copenhagen, her former home, could save their marriage and enable them to find happiness again.

In October 1884, Mette set off for Denmark with their five children. A month later, Gauguin joined them, bringing his art collection with him. Before leaving France, in order to insure some income, he had found work as the Danish representative for a manufacturer of waterproof canvas.

Life in Copenhagen was even worse than it had been in Rouen for Gauguin. Upon his arrival, he had been optimistic, trying his best to learn the new language and to sell enough canvas to support Mette and their children. But, in spite of his good intentions, Mette's family made life unbearable for him. They showed nothing but contempt for this so-called artist, who was un-able to make a living at his painting or at anything else. Soon Mette was forced to give French lessons and translate French novels in-to Danish for money.

Gauguin spent three months in Pont-Aven, Brittany, beginning in July 1886. There he found colorful, picturesque subjects, such as these women washing their clothes in the Aven, which inspired some of his finest early paintings.

239. PONT-AVEN — Les Laveuses - Vue sur l'Aven

Collection VILLARD, Quimper

Worst of all, Gauguin was unable to spend time painting. "I am more tormented by art here than ever," he wrote to his friend Schuffenecker in Paris, "my money difficulties as well as my searching for business cannot turn me from it. . . . I'm broke, fed up to the back teeth, that's why I console myself dreaming."

In May 1885, Gauguin complained in a letter to Pissarro that he was at the end of his courage and resources. "Every day I ask myself whether it wouldn't be better to go to the attic and put a rope around my neck," he wrote. "What prevents me from doing so is painting, yet here precisely lies the stumbling block. My wife, the family, everybody reproaches me for that confounded art, pretending that it is a disgrace not to earn one's living. But the faculties of a man cannot suffice for two things, and I can only do *one thing:* Paint. Everything else renders me stupid. . . ."

In June 1885, Gauguin returned to Paris accompanied by his six-year-old son Clovis. He was penniless and he had little hope of making a living. For one year he was completely dependent on the few friends who occasionally offered him hospitality and lent him money. In spite of his qualifications, he was unable to get any kind of job at the stock exchange. A position as assistant to a sculptor fell through when the sculptor's commission was canceled. And all of his efforts to sell his own paintings had failed; Paul Durand-Ruel, the courageous dealer who had helped the Impressionists in their early struggles and the only dealer he felt might take an interest in his work, was himself near financial ruin.

Guests and staff in front of the Gloanec Inn in Pont-Aven. Gauguin is seated in the front row, second from left.

As a result, Gauguin was not able to provide a home or even enough food for his young son. The two moved wearily from one rented room to another, carrying with them a trunk they had brought from Denmark. At times, Gauguin found friends who would take Clovis in for a week or two, but often the young boy slept on a rented bed, while his father, wrapped in a rug, slept on a mattress on the floor. At one point, all that Gauguin and his son had to eat was bread—and the bread had been bought on credit.

In December, near tragedy struck when Clovis took ill with smallpox, a potentially fatal disease. Fortunately, a generous neighbor looked after the boy, while Gauguin, desperate, found work hanging posters in a railroad station at a meager salary of five francs a day. Promotions followed—Gauguin was appointed inspector and then administrative secretary—and these eased their financial situation. This was only a temporary solution to his problem, however. Gauguin's mind was still first and foremost on his art.

Since his return to Paris, Gauguin had had little chance to paint and no opportunity to show his work. For this reason, he was preoccupied during the first months of 1886 with the first such opportunity—the forthcoming eighth Impressionist Exhibition. Perhaps the paintings he showed there would gain him the recognition and sales he so badly needed.

That exhibition, however, was in many ways a failure. The Impressionist movement was falling apart. Its members quarreled, and three of them—Renoir, Monet, and Sisley—even refused to take part in what was to be the last group exhibition. All attention that year was focused on the work of a new school of painters who had developed a technique known as Pointillism—the use of little specks of pure color which, when seen at a distance, blend in the eyes of the viewer. Because of the excitement, both favorable and unfavorable, generated by the masterpieces of this new movement, Gauguin's nineteen paintings and one wood-relief were ignored by most viewers.

When the eighth Impressionist Exhibition came to an end in June 1886, a year had passed since Gauguin had left his wife and four of their children in Copenhagen. During that year, the couple had corresponded only sporadically. Mette's letters revealed her anger and bitterness. Their marriage might possibly work, she felt, but only if he would give up the idea of making a living as an artist and return to the world of business. Though he, too, hoped for a reconciliation, Gauguin's letters were equally bitter. He accused his wife of living in luxury while he struggled to make ends meet. He felt that it was *he* who had been abandoned, that Mette had coldly rejected the man he really was—an artist.

During that year, despite the setbacks and humiliations, Gauguin never wavered from his devotion to his art. He never doubted that he would someday receive the recognition he deserved. His failure, he felt, could be blamed largely on the never ending struggle to overcome the economic and physical deprivations that consumed so much of his strength and energy. If only he could find the time to devote himself completely to his art . . .

Such a period came sooner than he had expected. In July, a generous loan from a distant relative enabled him, temporarily at least, to set aside his exhausting struggle to survive. After sending Clovis off to boarding school, he set out for Brittany, an isolated primitive region in northwest France. There he settled into the small picturesque village of Pont-Aven, about twelve miles from the dramatic, rocky coast of the Atlantic Ocean, where he hoped to remain for a few months.

Pont-Aven had, for some years, attracted to it artists from many parts of the world—America, Holland, England, and Scandinavia among them. Its appeal was obvious. A remote community of proud and somber farmers, millers, and fishermen, their way of life seemed untouched by modern civilization. A pious people, they observed their religious festivals as they had for centuries. The women continued to wear their native costumes—their smocks and bonnets and high lace headdresses. And, for a few francs, they would pose for visiting artists.

Because of these qualities, Pont-Aven provided the ideal setting for a painter eager to capture on canvas the character of a unique town, its citizens, and the gray, mysterious countryside that surrounded it. As a

This cylindrical vase, an example of the collaboration between Gauguin and the ceramist Ernest Chaplet, is dated 1886–87. The two figures in the foreground are based on a painting of four Breton women by the artist.

Paul Gauguin
Les Cigales et les fourmis

further attraction, living in Pont-Aven was inexpensive, especially for those who were fortunate to find a room at the inn owned by Marie-Hoanne Gloanec, who not only charged little rent but never insisted that artists pay their bills on time.

As soon as he arrived Gauguin took a room in the attic of the Gloanec Inn. For the first time in his life, he was free to live the life of a painter. Aloof and superior as ever, he made only one friend, a Frenchman named Charles Laval, who was fourteen years his junior. The other painters remained strangers to him; he kept his distance from them, usually keeping silent when in their company at the inn. He preferred to carve decorations on a walking stick or on a pair of clogs while the others passed their evenings in what he considered idle conversation.

A solitary figure, wearing a blue fisherman's jersey with a beret pulled over one ear, Gauguin became known as an eccentric, and not a very likable one.

Locusts and Ants, *one of ten lithographic drawings executed by Gauguin in 1889, offers evidence that the painter was able to master the use of a new medium—lithography—in a remarkably short time.*

But he was soon respected for the boldness and vitality of his art, which seemed revolutionary to most of the other painters in the village. Through them, he gained self-confidence and boasted to Mette, "I am respected as the best painter in Pont-Aven. . . . Everyone discusses my advice."

In the middle of October, this carefree period of creativity came to an end. It was time to return to Paris. Gauguin had benefited greatly from living among a quiet, simple people, whose culture differed in many ways from his own. By moving further away from the influence of Pissarro and the other Impressionists, his work began to develop a style which would, during his next stay in Pont-Aven, become truly his own.

Back in Paris, Gauguin learned quickly that he still could not make a living through his art alone. Faced with the need to support himself and Clovis who had returned from boarding school, he turned his hand to ceramics. But his attempts to "communicate to a vase the life of a figure, while retaining the character of the material," as he wrote, were as impossible to sell as were his paintings. His prospects were no better than they had been before he went to Brittany. Once again nearly destitute and unable to take care of his son, he wrote Mette that he had to escape and for the first time had dreamed of going away to a primitive place in a warm climate, where he could live inexpensively off the land. It was a dream that would haunt him for the rest of his life.

At the end of what had been a harsh and trying winter in Paris, he worked out a plan to make this dream come true. He would go to Panama, where he had relatives, and move to a small, sparsely inhabited island off the coast to live the simple life he so desperately needed.

In early April 1887, his wife arrived in Paris to take Clovis back to Copenhagen. A few days later, Gauguin, accompanied by Charles Laval, embarked for Panama. After a long, rough journey, the two men arrived at their destination. They learned quickly that they would have more trouble reaching "paradise" than they had expected, since Gauguin's relatives showed no interest in helping them. And they also learned that the island, where Gauguin hoped they could live like savages, "on fish and fruit for nothing . . . without anxiety for the day and for the morrow," had already been spoiled. The natives, anticipating an economic boom because of the building of the Panama Canal, had raised the price of land so that it was far beyond the reach of the two struggling artists.

One hope remained: to travel back to another island, Martinique, which they had seen on their way to Panama. The two men set out to earn enough money to pay for the trip—Laval by painting portraits, and Gauguin by working twelve-hour days helping to dig the Panama Canal.

A month later, they had earned the price of their passage to Martinique. Upon arrival, they rented an abandoned hut a few miles from the village of Saint Pierre. Soon, Gauguin realized that he had found the primitive island he had been looking for. The landscape, with its brilliant colors, and the warm, friendly natives delighted him. "I can't describe for you my enthusiasm for life in the French colonies," he wrote Mette. If only he could find an outlet in France for his paintings, he assured his wife, the whole family could join him in Martinique where they would live happily together.

Gauguin sent this sketch of one of his most famous paintings, The Vision after the Sermon, *to Vincent van Gogh in a letter of September 22, 1888.*

There was one serious flaw in what was otherwise an ideal existence. The island's damp tropical climate proved to be devastating for Gauguin. Already weakened from his journey from France and his exhausting physical labor on the Panama Canal, he developed dysentery and malaria. After four months, he had to return to France for medical treatment, leaving his hopes of finding a new life on Martinique behind. But all had not been lost. During his time on the island, he completed twenty luminous paintings in a style which would soon be recognized unmistakably as his own.

Chapter Four

The Decisive Years

Having worked his passage home as a deckhand on a schooner, Gauguin arrived in France in November 1887 without Laval, who remained in Martinique. Weak and thin, and still suffering from the effects of the illnesses, he was destitute, forced to seek refuge in the home of his old friend Schuff until he found his own small studio.

With very few exceptions, no one seemed interested in his paintings, but among those enthusiastic about his progress was a Dutch painter, Vincent van Gogh, whom he had met shortly before leaving for Panama. The two men were temperamentally very different. Gauguin was cool headed and reflective, while Van Gogh was more emotional and impulsive. But they had a great deal in common. Van Gogh, five years younger than Gauguin, had also taken up painting as a profession at the relatively late age of thirty, although he had drawn and sketched long before then. He, like Gauguin, was an artist with strong convictions, and both searched for new ways of expressing themselves through their art. They were, because of this, united by a feeling of isolation from the popular artistic movements of their time.

Van Gogh had come to Paris in 1886 to live with his devoted younger brother, Theo, who worked in an art gallery. Theo, a kind and gentle man, sold works of many contemporary painters. Sharing his brother's enthusiasm for Gauguin, he did his best to sell his paintings through his gallery. A few did sell—Theo himself bought three canvases—but the money earned

Tropical Vegetation. 1887

This painting with a view of the bay of Saint-Pierre was painted during Gauguin's stay in Martinique. The volcano, Mount Pelée, can be seen in the background.

was not nearly enough to support Gauguin. The best solution for the debt-ridden artist was to return to Pont-Aven, where he could live cheaply and take advantage of the generosity of Madame Gloanec.

Life in Pont-Aven was difficult during the winter of 1888. The climate was harsh and the town was deserted. Members of the art world only visited during the spring and summer. Gauguin's health had not yet returned to normal, and he was sometimes so poor that he couldn't afford canvas and paints. He also worried about his family in Denmark; he had still not given up hope of a reconciliation. In March, desperately lonely, he wrote to Mette: "All alone in the room of an inn from morning till night, I have absolute silence, nobody with whom I can exchange ideas." Yet he believed that his art would reach its maturity in Pont-Aven. "I like Brittany, it is savage and primitive," he wrote to Schuff. "The flat sound of my wooden clogs on the cobblestones, deep, hollow, and powerful, is the note I seek in my painting."

During this period, he kept in contact with Theo and Vincent van Gogh. The former continued to try to sell his paintings, but he had little luck. Vincent wrote to Gauguin of his hopes to form an artists' cooperative to help promote and sell their work. He suggested, too, that Gauguin come to live and work with him in Arles, in the south of France, where they would be joined later by other struggling artists.

At first, Gauguin ignored this suggestion. But in the late spring Theo came forth with a new and more feasible plan. Having just received a small unexpected inheritance, the art dealer offered Gauguin a fixed monthly allowance in exchange for one painting per month—on the condition that he agree to join Vincent in Arles. The two men could keep one another company, while sharing expenses. This time Gauguin accepted the offer, agreeing to come to Arles as soon as he had settled his debts to Madame Gloanec and to his doctor.

He was, however, in no hurry to leave Pont-Aven. As the warm weather returned to Brittany and visiting painters took up temporary residence in what had become a summer art colony, Pont-Aven again came to life. Gauguin acquired a following of younger artists who came to look upon him as their teacher and leader. It was a role he enjoyed, a recognition of his power and strength as a painter.

Part of the credit for his growth as an artist during this period must be given to Emile Bernard, a young Frenchman (he was only twenty years old at the time) who arrived in Pont-Aven in August. The two found they had a great deal in common. Bernard was as profoundly interested in literature, music, and philosophy as he was in art. He and the older painter, whom he looked to as his master, soon became close friends and colleagues, enthusiastically working together and discussing their theories of art and their methods of painting. It became clear that they had, independent of one another, reached similar conclusions. Their goals were the same: to express their inner feelings and visions through their painting rather than to depict

Early Flowers in Brittany. *1888*

This light-filled landscape, painted at Pont-Aven in the springtime, was greatly admired by Degas, who considered purchasing it when it was exhibited in Paris.

reality or portray nature like the Impressionists. Gauguin wrote Schuff: "Don't copy nature too literally. Art is abstraction; draw art from nature as you dream in nature's presence."

To reach these goals, Gauguin and Bernard developed a new style, which came to be known as Symbolism or Synthetism. Influenced by Japanese prints, as well as folk art, tapestries, and ancient frescoes, their paintings rejected traditional perspective and made use of brilliant flat col-

The Vision after the Sermon (Jacob Wrestling with the Angel). *1888*
A group of Breton women pray devoutly while a vision of a story from the book of Genesis in the Bible appears before them. Gauguin's first Symbolist painting and said to be the first work painted entirely from his imagination, it makes use of many elements of this new style.

Old Women at Arles. *1888*

This work shows two women protecting themselves with their shawls against the harsh wind, as they walk through a public garden opposite the house Van Gogh shared with Gauguin. The women, Gauguin wrote Emile Bernard, reminded him of the women found in the processions on Greek urns.

ors, bounded by heavy black outlines that defined and intensified these areas of color, creating two-dimensional objects and figures.

The few months spent working with Bernard were exciting ones, artistically, for Gauguin. During this period, he created some of his most vibrant and beautiful works. In early autumn, this productive period came to an end. Bernard had to return to Paris and Gauguin felt it was time to accept Theo's offer.

At the end of October 1888, after sending a number of his works to Theo in Paris, Gauguin arrived in Arles. Vincent eagerly awaited his arrival. He had furnished the house they would live in and painted decorations in Gauguin's bedroom. He was certain that his friend would remain with him for at least one year, during which time they would attract other artists to Arles and form an artists' studio. Gauguin had other ideas; he expected to stay in Arles for six months. After that, he planned to leave France again and resume his quest for paradise on an island in the tropics.

Both men, however, were apparently unaware of the profound differences between them that would bring their experiment in shared living to a dramatic end after only two months. The neat and well-organized Gauguin was horrified by the sloppiness and disorder he found in Van Gogh's home. Though Gauguin did his best to put the house in order, plan the meals (which he cooked), and establish a workable budget, the Dutch painter remained unconcerned with such matters. Gauguin, too, found Arles itself, which Van Gogh loved so much, to be the "dirtiest town in the South." He found that its women and landscapes lacked the fascination and mystery of Brittany and its inhabitants. Though they admired each other's paintings, they disagreed in matters of art as well. "Our arguments are terribly electric," Vincent wrote to Theo. "We come out of them sometimes with our heads as exhausted as an electric battery, after it is discharged."

Tensions between the two men increased rapidly. In the middle of December, Gauguin completed a portrait of Vincent painting sunflowers. "It is certainly I," Vincent commented. "But it is I gone mad." This was a startling prediction of events to come.

The decisive event took place on the evening of December 23. As Gauguin was taking a walk through the town gardens, he heard footsteps behind him and found Van Gogh wildly menacing him with a razor. Able to ward him off, he spent the night in a local hotel while Van Gogh returned home. The following morning, Gauguin found Van Gogh curled up in bed under blood-stained sheets. After an investigation, it was determined that the previous evening, after the two men had separated, the deeply troubled Dutch painter turned the razor on himself, cutting off the lower part of his left ear which he delivered to a local prostitute. Because he bled so profusely, it was a miracle that he was still alive.

Gauguin summoned Theo immediately to Arles to care for his brother. On Christmas morning, badly shaken by the experience, he left for Paris.

Gauguin's stay in Arles had been shorter than he had anticipated, and it had ended tragically. In spite of this, he had worked well there, completing several new canvases, including the moving portrait of Van Gogh and a haunting painting, *Old Women at Arles*.

Upon his return to the French capital, he was once again faced with the problem that had plagued him ever since he had made the decision to pur-

---

Van Gogh Painting Sunflowers. 1888

Vincent van Gogh had a premonition of his emotional breakdown when he told Gauguin that he looked mad in this portrait. He also wrote his brother, Theo, that he "looked extremely tired and charged with electricity." The next evening in a café, the Dutch painter threw a glass of absinthe at Gauguin's head.

sue his career as an artist. He desperately needed money. And his paintings were not selling, in spite of Theo's continued efforts on his behalf. Because of his brother's illness and the failure of the projected artists' studio, the kind dealer was no longer able to send Gauguin his monthly stipend. He promised to try to sell his work through his gallery, and even agreed to advance the painter money against the future sale of his works.

Gauguin returned to Brittany, profoundly discouraged after little more than a month in Paris. He was to spend almost all of the next two years there, working with his customary dedication and hoping, through his art, to make enough money to be able to escape to his paradise island. And he knew that a reconciliation with his family would have to wait until he could return as a successful, prosperous artist.

During these years there were reasons to hope and reasons to despair. Most important, Gauguin needed opportunities to show his work, and these opportunities rarely presented themselves. All of Paris was excited in the spring of 1889 about the forthcoming World's Fair, celebrating the hun-

(left) The Dutchman Jacob Meyer de Haan, the subject of this 1889 watercolor (a study for a larger oil), joined Gauguin in Brittany in 1889. The two painters became close friends.

(right) This jug is a self-portrait of the artist. One of his most famous ceramic works, it was the first of his creations to enter a public collection, the Museum of Decorative Arts in Copenhagen.

dredth anniversary of the French Revolution. As part of this celebration, art was to be displayed in a new exhibition hall, not far from the recently completed Eiffel Tower. Not surprisingly, however, only those painters who were officially accepted were asked to show their work and Gauguin was not one of them. Disappointed not to have the chance to show his work, Gauguin was delighted when his friend Schuff came up with what turned out to be the ideal site for an independent exhibition: the large hall of a café located right next to the official art section of the Fair.

When this news reached Gauguin at Pont-Aven, he immediately sent a list of works that he wanted included in the exhibition. He also requested that forty other paintings be shown, works by Bernard, Schuffenecker, and Van Gogh among them. "It's *our* show," he wrote Schuff in refusing to include paintings by Pissarro, with whom he no longer wanted to be associated, and Seurat.

In the middle of April, Gauguin came to Paris to supervise the exhibition. He worked energetically, even helping to carry the canvases, framed in white at his request, to the café. Almost one hundred paintings, drawings, and watercolors were hung, including seventeen of his own.

In spite of his efforts, the exhibition was not a success. It attracted little attention, and none of the works shown was sold. There was some compensation for Gauguin: He had an opportunity to visit the many exotic pavilions at the Fair, and many of the young artists who saw his work recognized Gauguin as the leader of a new and exciting movement.

Though he valued the recognition he had received, Gauguin returned to Pont-Aven in June deeply discouraged. He saw little hope of raising money to leave France, and he was depressed by what he found at Pont-Aven. The small, quaint, isolated artists' colony had changed. It was now filled with mediocre, popular artists, as well as crowds of noisy, curious tourists. Within a short time, he moved to the much smaller and far less crowded village of Le Pouldu, situated on a bleak and dramatic stretch of coast, ten miles from Pont-Aven.

The move to Le Pouldu proved to be a wise one, artistically, for Gauguin. The other residents at the fishermen's inn where he lived included many gifted painters who had followed him there. Among these were his

Yellow Christ. *1889*

This is one of the most important examples of Gauguin's Synthetism, and it was a powerful influence on Gauguin's disciples. The flat unmodeled yellow, the artist said, was intended to express the feelings he had about the desolate isolation and medieval quality of life in Brittany.

La Belle Angèle (Portrait of Marie-Angélique Satre). *1889*
When the artist allowed the subject, the wife of the mayor of Pont-Aven, to see this
portrait, she called it a "horror" and refused to keep it in her home.

old friend Laval and Jacob Meyer de Haan, a Dutch painter with whom Gauguin shared a studio and who, most important, shared his generous allowance with him from his family in Amsterdam. These men lived for their art; they painted during the day and engaged in stimulating discussions at night. Gauguin proved to be an inspiration to them, as he had to other young artists in the past.

Some of Gauguin's finest paintings were created during this period, works that reflected his interest in the activities of the simple peasants of Brittany, like *The Seaweed Gatherers*, and in the religious life of the Bretons, notably *Yellow Christ*, a masterpiece inspired by a seventeenth-century wooden figure of Christ. Nonetheless, the struggle continued, unabated. "Since January," he wrote Emile Bernard, "my sales have totaled 925 francs. At the age of forty-two, to live on that, to buy colors, etc., is enough to daunt the stoutest heart. It is not so much the privations now as that the future difficulties loom so high when we are low. In the face of living, even meanly, I do not know what to do."

More and more, finding the means to reach his island in paradise became Gauguin's obsession. In February 1890, Gauguin traveled to Paris to convince the French colonial department to appoint him on a mission to the French protectorate of Tonkin, in what is now Vietnam. When that effort failed, he turned his hopes of escape to the island of Madagascar, in the Indian Ocean. He planned to form a studio of the tropics there—much like Van Gogh's aborted studio of the south. He would live like a "savage peasant," while Theo, in Paris, would sell his older paintings as well as any new works he would create there. By May, he felt his dream might become a reality when a wealthy admirer, Dr. Charlopin, an inventor, offered to purchase thirty-eight paintings and five ceramic pots for a sum that would more than cover the expenses of this trip.

Genuinely hopeful for the first time, Gauguin returned the next month to Brittany. But his optimism was short-lived, and soon everything began to fall apart. On August 1, he learned that Vincent van Gogh had shot himself a few days earlier and had died in his brother's arms on July 29. Theo, distraught, admitted himself to a clinic two months later, and his retirement from the gallery was announced shortly afterward. Gauguin had lost two of his staunchest supporters.

In desperation, he traveled to Paris in early November, only to learn that Dr. Charlopin no longer intended to buy his paintings. Art galleries, too, disappointed him, showing absolutely no interest in his work. Without Theo, his gallery Boussod and Valadon no longer cared to make any efforts on his part; on the contrary, the new director asked Gauguin to take back the paintings he had left there on consignment. Furthermore, he learned that none of his friends and colleagues would be able to join him in his escape to paradise.

Nonetheless, Gauguin was determined to pursue his goal. Madagascar no longer interested him—he feared that it was too close to the civilized world. Instead, he planned to go to the island of Tahiti, a French colony in the Pacific, and he was willing to do everything in his power to get there. If Parisian galleries were unable to sell his paintings, he would sell them himself at auction. But he needed help to make such an auction successful.

Gauguin's arrogance had, through the years, lost him some good friends. Nonetheless, he still had faithful allies, especially the Symbolist writers who were becoming increasingly influential in France. These writers, among them Stéphane Mallarmé, Paul Verlaine, and Arthur Rimbaud, did with words what the artist did with colors and shapes: they suggested and evoked ideas and feelings rather than documenting reality. Looking upon him as the leader of Symbolist painting, they were eager to take up his cause by praising him as an unrecognized genius in newspaper and magazine articles. As a result of their efforts, the auction of Gauguin's works, held February 23, was a success. The artist earned more from this auction than if the transaction from Dr. Charlopin had been concluded.

At last Gauguin was able to make concrete plans for his departure. He

---

Self-Portrait with Halo. *1889*
This provocative self-portrait was painted directly on the wooden cupboard doors in the dining room of Marie Henry's inn at Le Pouldu. It was conceived as a caricature, and the artist portrayed himself as the Fallen Angel.

The Seaweed Gatherers. *1889*

Gauguin wrote in a letter to Van Gogh: "I see this scene every day, and it is like a gust of wind, a sudden awareness of the struggle for life, of sadness, and of our obedience to the harsh laws of nature."

traveled to Copenhagen on March 7 for what he hoped might be a favorable meeting with his family, but it was difficult—of his children, only the two oldest spoke any French, and he was unable to communicate well with the others. His visit with Mette, however, was apparently a successful one. She would not go to Tahiti with him, but she tentatively agreed to join him when he returned to Europe in three years, the time needed to complete new work and hold a one-man exhibition in Paris.

Shortly after his return to Paris further good news reached him. Largely through the efforts of Charles Morice, a Symbolist poet, Gauguin had been granted funds for an official art mission to Tahiti. This meant a reduction in fare to the island, the guarantee of a respectful reception, as well as a commitment by the French government to purchase, for a large sum, a painting upon his return.

On April 1, 1891, Gauguin sailed for Tahiti. He took with him two mandolins and a guitar (he enjoyed playing both instruments), as well as a French horn and a shotgun—the last two were to be used to attract and kill wild game. Among his belongings, too, were what he called a "community of comrades." These included a large collection of prints, photos, and reproductions of Greek and Egyptian art, Renaissance and Baroque paintings, Japanese prints, and contemporary art.

The Haystacks, *or* ***The Potato Field.*** *1890*
This is one of a series of landscapes painted by Gauguin during his stay
at Marie Henry's inn in 1890. It is an example of what can be considered the
classic Pont-Aven style.

Chapter Five

To Tahiti and Back

Gauguin arrived in Papeete, Tahiti's capital, a city of over three thousand inhabitants, on June 9, 1891. His appearance—his shoulder-length hair, his brown velvet suit, and his cowboy hat—amused the natives, who nicknamed him *taata-vahine* (man-woman). He was greeted as a celebrity by officials of the French colony, who looked forward to the arrival of a distinguished artist. Based on their reception (and after quickly cutting his hair and buying a white colonial suit), he was certain that he could begin his Tahitian sojourn with lucrative portrait commissions from the colonists and the French soldiers among whom he mingled.

Before long, however, it was obvious that few such commissions would be forthcoming. His unconventional style did not please the conservative men and women who wanted only flattering portraits, nor did the often haughty behavior of the artist himself. Furthermore, it had been clear from the very beginning that Papeete was anything but the enchanting village of his dreams. Once known for its picturesque charm, its streets were lined with rows of undistinguished Western-style stores and ugly brick buildings. The French influence had extended to the once colorful Tahitians as well, who now imitated their colonizers by dressing in European clothing, replacing native garb. "It was," he wrote, "Europe—the Europe I thought I had finished with—in a form even worse, with colonial snobbery and aping of our

---

Tahitian Women, *or* ***On the Beach.*** *1891*
The artist superbly captures the languid, melancholy personality of these Tahitian women. It has been suggested that the same woman served as model for both of the women in this mysterious work.

(right) **Where Do We Come From? What Are We? Where Are We Going?** *1897*
This immense painting—more than twelve feet wide—is considered by many scholars to be Gauguin's masterpiece. In February 1898, the artist wrote to his painter-friend Monfreid: "I put into it all my energy, such aching passion . . . and vision so clear, needing no correction, that all sense of hurried execution vanishes, and it surges with life. . . ."

Nevermore. *1897*

The artist wrote to Monfreid in 1897: "I wished to suggest by means of a simple nude a certain long lost barbaric luxury. It is completely drowned in colors which are deliberately somber and sad; it is neither silk, nor velvet, nor muslin, nor gold that creates this luxury but simply the material made rich by the artist. . . . Man's imagination alone has enriched the dwelling with his fantasy."

customs, fashions, vices, and crazes in a manner so grotesque that it bordered on caricature."

In September, three months after his arrival, Gauguin was eager to find a home in the legendary Tahiti of the past. He left Papeete and settled in the district of Mataiea, thirty miles down the coast. Life there, too, had been greatly influenced by missionaries, traders, and sailors from Europe. Nevertheless, Gauguin found the district far more interesting and more beautiful than the Europeanized, unappealing town of Papeete; its population of 516 lived in fifty huts and houses scattered among the palm trees. The view from his hut was breathtaking: the dazzling blue water, the countryside thick with coconut palms, breadfruits, and ironwood trees. The people, too, were delightful—warm, cheerful, and hospitable.

It seemed, at first, idyllic, and once he grew accustomed to the intense light and colors that initially blinded him (he was used to the somber shades of Brittany), Gauguin began to work. At first he drew what he called "documents," or scenes of everyday life, and figure studies, largely of women. These drawings depicted a land and a people of exceptional beauty. Ignoring the flaws and the realities of the Tahiti he saw, the artist showed the land and people of his imagination.

By early 1892 he was forced to recognize the difficulties and hardships which had plagued him since he had come to live in Mataiea. His greatest problem, once again, was his inability to earn enough money to support himself. The funds he had brought with him from France had quickly run out, and he received neither money nor news regarding payment from the sale of his paintings in Paris. Life on the island was indeed inexpensive, but only for the natives who knew how to catch fish and wild boar, and who were experienced in gathering fruit from the trees. Gauguin, for a long time, subsisted on little more than bread and fruit, since the food at the stores

Vahine no te vi (Woman with a Mango). 1892
This portrait of a radiant, voluptuous Tahitian woman, holding
a ripe mango in her right hand, is almost too pleasing. Yet, it is distinguished by
the artist's rich, vibrant colors.

was far beyond his means.

During these months, too, Gauguin had become ill. Hospitalized after starting to spit up blood, he was told by doctors that he had suffered a heart attack. Unable to pay his bills, he left the hospital against their orders.

By May, the situation had worsened, as the artist's health, because of his inadequate diet, deteriorated. Yet he was stubbornly determined to finish his work. He considered moving on to the Marquesas Islands, about 750 miles northeast of Tahiti, where he could live among an unspoiled, primitive people. But even the small amount of money he needed to reach there was

The Siesta. c. 1891–92
This large canvas lacks a signature, date, and title, but it is believed to have been painted in France after Gauguin's first visit to Tahiti. It shows Tahitians—doing household work and sitting at leisure—in a colonial setting. The colonial influence is reflected in the women's clothing and the structure of the veranda.

impossible to raise, and this plan was abandoned.

In June, Gauguin's first year in Tahiti came to an end. He had finished thirty-five paintings and made hundreds of sketches from which he could later create finished works of art. It was an important body of work, but he had hoped to accomplish even more before going home. He didn't have enough money to remain on the island, and he didn't have enough to pay his passage to France. In desperation, he wrote an official letter to Paris, pleading penury and requesting that he be repatriated at the government's expense. It would take at least four months to receive a reply to his request,

---

(left) **Ia Orana Maria (Hail Mary).** *1891–92*
The artist described the intensely religious painting to his friend Monfreid
as an angel with yellow wings pointing out Mary and Jesus, shown as Tahitians, to
two Tahitian women. "I am rather pleased with it."

(below) A photograph showing native huts, taken in 1891, the year Gauguin first
arrived in Tahiti. The artist probably lived in a similar hut while in Mataiea.

so he continued to work the best he could to capture on canvas his vision of Tahiti and its people.

His work, he knew, had suffered over the past months. Preoccupied with a need to earn money, he had not yet fully understood the natives among whom he lived. To remedy this, he undertook a trip through the more primitive parts of the island, hoping to gain greater insight into the character of the Tahitians, and hoping, too, to find a *vahine,* or woman, with whom to live. Such arrangements—westerners living with young Tahitian women—were common on the island and were not considered immoral.

Manao tupapau (Spirit of the Dead Watching). *1892*

Gauguin wrote of this complex masterpiece: "The musical composition: undulating lines, harmonies of orange and blue connected by the secondary colors of yellow and violet, and lit by greenish sparks. The literary theme: the soul of the living woman united with the spirit of the dead. The opposites of night and day.

. . . I have set down the origin of this picture for those who must know the why and the wherefore. But otherwise it is simply a nude from the South Seas."

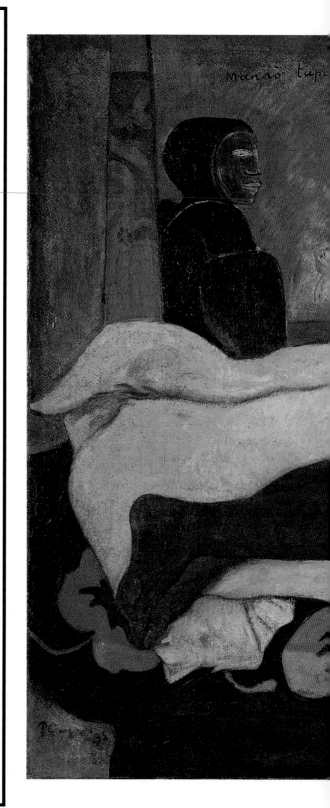

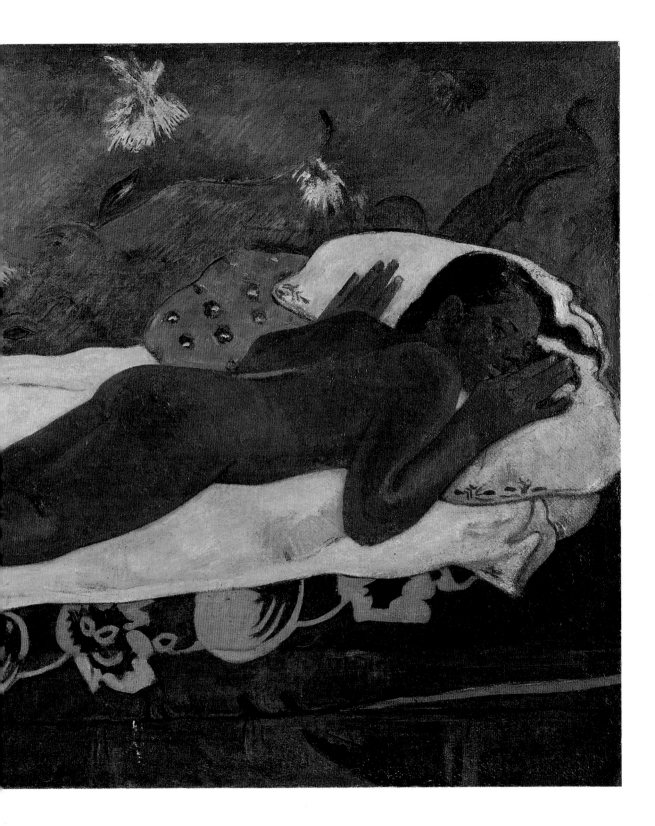

His trip was successful in every way, and he returned to Mataiea with a thirteen-year-old *vahine* named Tehamana. The young girl was all he could have hoped for. Beautiful, gentle, and sweet, she took care of the artist, assuming all the household chores and bringing to his life all the joy he had been missing for such a long time. Gauguin began to work well again, painting numerous portraits of Tehamana, as well as richly colored, vibrant scenes of everyday life.

Nonetheless, his struggles continued. A letter from Mette informed him of a forthcoming exhibition of his work in Copenhagen and that she had managed to sell a few of his paintings. Yet no money was on its way. Mette wrote that she needed the money for herself and the children, and Morice, his collector, remained silent. "Farewell, hospitable land, country of freedom and beauty. I leave two years older but twenty years younger," he wrote, referring to his departure from Tahiti, completely ignoring the poverty and illness he had experienced during much of his stay on the island.

When Gauguin arrived in France on August 30, 1893, he was certain that his hopes would be realized. In spite of all of his problems, he had worked hard in Tahiti and had completed more than sixty paintings. These works would, assuredly, finally bring him the recognition he deserved. With it, financial rewards would follow and allow him to be reunited with his wife and children.

Before long, however, he realized that his prospects were no brighter than they had been when he set off for Tahiti. Mette wrote saying that the Copenhagen exhibition had been a failure financially, and that no money would be forthcoming. Government officials conveniently forgot their promise to buy one of his paintings upon his return from Tahiti. The only

---

Merahi metua no Tehamana (Tehamana Has Many Parents). *1893*
This dignified portrait of Gauguin's thirteen-year-old vahine *holding a palm fan was painted in the months before Gauguin's return to France in 1893. The title refers both to the Tahitian custom of real and foster parents sharing children and to the belief that all Tahitians are descendants from the union of two dieties.*

Self-Portrait with Hat. *1893–94*

Painted in his Parisian studio, this self-portrait shows the artist in front of Manao
tupapau, *one of his favorite works. The latter is reversed—an indication that
Gauguin painted this scene while looking in a mirror.*

good financial news came from Orléans, where the artist's uncle had died, leaving him a generous inheritance. That money would not be available to him for several months, however, until all legal matters concerning the will had been settled. In the meantime, Gauguin would have to depend on the charity and generosity of friends.

All was not hopeless, for shortly after his arrival in Paris, the artist was promised a large exhibition of his work, to be held at Durand-Ruel's gallery. The dealer offered the space and prestige of his gallery, while Gauguin was responsible for organizing and financing the entire exhibition, which would open in just two months. It was an enormous job, and Gauguin called upon his old friend, Charles Morice, for help. Morice was forgiven for failing him while he was in Tahiti, and he promised to write an introduction to the catalogue and to use his influence in getting the publicity that was essential to the success of the exhibition. Morice also agreed to work with the painter on a book that would explain the meaning and background of these new paintings.

Preparations went smoothly, and the exhibition opened on November 9. It consisted of forty-one paintings from Tahiti, three from Brittany, and two sculptures. Public response was disappointing. Many viewers were shocked by the dazzling bright colors and the unfamiliar subject matter. According to one journalist, an Englishwoman let out a scream of horror when viewing the image of a red dog. And many visitors to the gallery laughed derisively at the titles of the paintings, most of them in Tahitian.

The reaction of the press was more encouraging. Though some critics were disconcerted by the artist's use of "unnatural" colors and made fun of his yellow seas and purple trees, many were impressed by his progress and achievements. The young people, as well as the writers, poets, and intellectuals, were the most enthusiastic, and one of their leaders, the great French Symbolist poet Stéphane Mallarmé, expressed the feelings of many when he wrote: "It is extraordinary that so much mystery can be put into so much brilliance."

In spite of this praise, the exhibition was a failure financially. When it closed on November 25, only eleven paintings had been sold, barely covering the artist's expenses. Nonetheless, Gauguin was heartened by the attention he had received. "My exhibition did not actually achieve the results that was expected of it," he wrote Mette. "Never mind. The main thing is that my show was a very great artistic success, even arousing fury and jealousy. . . . For the moment, many people consider me the greatest modern painter."

Mette, however, was not interested in his "artistic success." Tired of what she considered his selfish behavior, she had had enough of his dreams and promises. She wanted only one thing from him: money. The tone of her letters in return made it obvious that she no longer loved the man she had married and, as far as she was concerned, there was absolutely no hope of a reconciliation.

Gauguin, too, was forced to face the fact that his marriage was over. However, his other dream—that of earning a good living as an artist—might still be fulfilled. Through the exhibition, he had gained a measure of fame, at least among Parisian intellectuals. Now he would devote his time to firmly establishing his reputation as an artist and to explaining his "exotic" paintings to the public, hoping to make them easier to sell.

Gauguin set about his task energetically. In January, little more than a month after the close of the exhibition, he received a legacy from his uncle, and with it he rented two large rooms on the top floor of a building on Paris's Left Bank, where most of the artists lived. Having established a reputation as an eccentric painter of unconventional works, he decided to live like one. He painted the walls of his studio chrome yellow and olive green, and covered them with paintings of his own and of those artists he admired. He filled the room with fabulous objects—spears, wood carvings, Australian boomerangs, and intricately carved furniture—which he acquired during his travels. No longer a family man, he duplicated his Tahitian way of life by sharing his home with a Javanese thirteen-year-old girl, Annah, and her small monkey, Taoa.

Each Thursday night, he held court in his lavishly decorated studio, playing host to painters, poets, and musicians. Together they sang songs and played music, and often Gauguin would regale them with stories of his travels and share his ideas on art. He became a colorful and increasingly well known figure in the world of art in Paris.

During these months, Gauguin spent little time painting. Instead, he devoted his time to completing *Noa Noa*, meaning "fragrant land," the book he hoped would explain the Tahitian images in his paintings. Written in collaboration with Charles Morice, *Noa Noa* is an account of the artist's stay in Tahiti, a mixture of fact and fiction. Some of it, including an entire chapter on Tahitian mythology, is copied word for word from an earlier Belgian account of the religious beliefs and customs of Tahiti. But it is in some ways an enchantingly poetic work. To illustrate it, Gauguin created ten superb woodcuts, which he himself carved and then

This photo, showing the artist wearing a Breton jacket, was taken in 1891, the year he left on his first trip to Tahiti.

printed in his Parisian bedroom during February and March of 1894.

In April, after his work on *Noa Noa* was completed, Gauguin was free to leave Paris and set off for Brittany. This attempt to recapture his past was a complete failure, and his stay there was a disastrous one. Neither Pont-Aven nor Le Pouldu inspired him as they once had and he found it difficult to paint. He was forced to stay in Brittany, however, far longer than he wanted to. On May 25, while visiting the small fishing village of Concarneau with Annah and a few friends, he became involved in a brawl with a number of local fishermen who had insulted Annah. In the course of the fight, he fell, breaking his right leg just above the ankle. Because of his injury, the artist was unable to walk, or paint, all summer. The intense pain was reduced only by alcohol and morphine, and Gauguin became profoundly depressed. As he lay in bed day after day, he made a decision: he would return to Tahiti. "Ever since I experienced the simple life of Oceania, I can think of only one thing: living far away from other people," he wrote Schuffenecker. "Europeans are unremittingly hostile to me; those good savages will understand me."

On November 14, he returned to Paris. When he entered his studio, he found that it had been ransacked by Annah. The young girl had taken everything she considered to be of value—leaving behind only Gauguin's paintings. In a final, desperate move to sell these remaining works of art, the artist opened his studio to the public for one week, beginning December 2. The art—watercolors, paintings, sculptures, and woodcuts, including the illustrations for *Noa Noa*—was viewed with interest by many of the artists, writers, and collectors who attended the informal exhibition. However, he was once again unable to raise the money he badly needed to go to Tahiti.

At a dinner held at the Café Escoffier, Gauguin announced that he would leave for Tahiti as soon as possible. "Paul Gauguin had to choose between the savages here or the ones over there; without a moment's hesitation, he will leave for Tahiti," the *Journal des Artistes* reported on December 16. In a final effort, the painter once again offered his works at public auction. The auction, held on February 18, was poorly attended, and only eight works were sold. Disheartened and bitter, he sailed for Tahiti on July 3. His departure had been delayed by a skin ailment that covered his whole body, labeled an "unfortunate disease" most probably syphilis.

Upaupa Schneklud (The Player Schneklud). *1894*

Fritz Schneklud was among those who attended the weekly musical and literary gatherings held in Paris by Gauguin in 1894. When working on this painting, the artist probably referred to a photograph of the cellist as a younger man. Curiously, the portrait closely resembles Gauguin himself.

Chapter Six

Exile

When Gauguin left for Tahiti in 1895, he had no specific, limited mission in mind, as he had had four years earlier. This time, he was convinced of the futility of his existence in Europe, and he was returning to his tropical paradise as a permanent settler.

When he arrived in Papeete, on September 9, 1895, he was reminded at once that the capital could hardly be described as a paradise. If anything, it was worse than he remembered it, more civilized and more Westernized. Had it not been for his few friends and the proximity of relatively decent medical care, he would have left at once for the more primitive Marquesas Islands.

Fortunately, in spite of his initial discouragement, he soon found what he hoped might be the ideal place to live—the small district of Punaauia, eight miles from the capital, where he rented a small plot of land on which he had a traditional oval Tahitian hut built of bamboo canes and palm leaves. His optimism returned briefly, as he settled in among the coconut palms, guavas, and banana trees, not far from the white beach that ran along the nearby lagoon.

During most of his first year there, he had to face the realities of his situation. He was, as he had been throughout his previous stay on the island, very much dependent on money and on news from Paris. He was alone and

---

The Young Christian Girl. *1894*

This small portrait was painted during the artist's last stay in Brittany. The red-haired model is believed to be the mistress of Monfreid. Of special interest is the yellow missionary dress which Gauguin must have brought to France from Tahiti.

isolated and, inevitably, home-sick. Tehamana, his former *vahine,* was married and no longer cared to live with a sick man whom she considered old. Her replacement as his *vahine* was the fourteen-year-old Pahura, who had neither the intelligence nor the compassion of her predecessor. Furthermore, Gauguin was once again seriously ill and out of money, unable to afford either painkillers or the medical attention he badly needed.

His condition, both emotional and physical, deteriorated throughout the first half of 1896. In April, profoundly depressed, he wrote Morice that he was contemplating suicide. By July, his body covered with sores, he was admitted to the hospital, officially listed as an indigent person. After a brief stay there, he left feeling almost miracu-

---

Mahana no atua (Day of the God). 1894

This fascinating allegorical work brings to life an ancient Tahitian religious festival. Though the subject is Tahitian, the artist painted it from memory while in Paris.

lously better. He began to paint enthusiastically, completing some of his most beautiful works, among them the monumental canvas *No te aha oe riri*. He sent his works back to Paris, whenever possible, with the hope that they might be sold. In December, good news arrived from France. He received a sizable check from a dealer who had been selling his works there, with the promise of more and larger checks to follow. Able, at last, to pay his debts and resume his work, he could face the future with a degree of serenity unknown to him for many years.

In April 1897 Gauguin's sense of well-being was brutally shattered when a short, abrupt letter from Mette informed him that their twenty-year-old daughter, Aline, had died of pneumonia on January 19. Of all his children, Aline was the closest to him in temperament, the one he felt had been unfairly neglected by Mette for this very reason. Distraught, he wrote to Mette: "I have just lost my daughter. I no longer love God. . . . Her tomb over there with flowers—it is only an illusion. Her tomb is here near me; my tears are her flowers; they are living things." This letter marked the end of his correspondence and relationship with Mette.

More disturbing (but less tragic) news reached Gauguin at the end of April. The man from whom he had rented the land on which he had built his hut had died, and his heirs were forced to sell the property and destroy the artist's home. Desperate, he borrowed money from the bank and bought another plot of land, near his former home, and added a large studio to an already existing wooden house.

The joy he found in his new home—far sturdier and more comfortable than his previous one—was not enough to raise Gauguin out of despair. His health worsened steadily, and his skin rash became so ugly that many of the natives shunned him for fear he had leprosy. Because of a serious eye infection, he was no longer able to paint as he had before, and he soon became obsessed with the idea of death. On September 30, he wrote to Georges-Daniel de Monfreid, a painter who shared his love of the sea and would remain his only loyal friend in France: "My journey to Tahiti was a mad adventure, but it has turned out to be sad and miserable. I see no way out except death, which solves all problems . . ."

In October, Gauguin suffered a series of minor heart attacks. In

December, a serious one forced him to confront death, whether by suicide or from natural causes. He decided to make one last enormous effort, to begin work on a major painting that would stand as a "testament," a summary of his spiritual and philosophical ideas. Painting directly on a huge, rough canvas, he worked feverishly day and night for several weeks to create the work he hoped would be his masterpiece. When it was completed, toward the end of the month, he titled it *Where Do We Come From? What Are We? Where Are We Going?*

Having made his final statement, he was determined to end his own life, before it was consumed by disease. With a box of powdered arsenic in his pocket, he climbed a nearby mountain to find a place to die alone, in peace, like a wounded animal. But the quantity of arsenic he took was too great, and the induced vomiting made him expel the poison. The following morning, after a night of intense suffering, he managed to make his way down the mountain.

Gauguin's failed attempt at suicide marked the beginning of the final phase of his life. He remained on Tahiti for almost four more tragic years, characterized by loneliness, anger, and intense physical suffering.

He painted only sporadically during those years, impeded by his steadily deteriorating health. His eyesight continued to fail, the sores on his body spread, and the wounds on his ankle,

Oviri (Savage). 1894

Considered by critics to be Gauguin's greatest ceramic work, the artist described Oviri *as ceramic sculpture. Hurt by his failure to find a buyer for it, he wrote: "I believe that one day the world will be more grateful to me. At all events, I proudly maintain that nobody has ever done this before."*

which had never healed properly, caused such pain that he was frequently unable to walk or stand before an easel.

Frustrated with not being able to paint often, he turned to journalism, venting his rage at the colonial government, first through bitter, combative essays written for a satirical journal, *Les Guêpes (The Wasps)*, and later for *Le Sourire (The Smile)*, a booklet that he wrote, edited, and printed himself.

Financial worries, too, continued to plague him, and he often had no money for canvas or colors. Eager to pay back the debts he had incurred in order to purchase the land for his new home, he took a position for almost a year as a draftsman in the Office of Public Works in Papeete. It was poorly paid, demeaning work, but he was determined to remain at his job until he was finally able to pay back his creditors.

In 1900, for the first time since his return to Tahiti, Gauguin had reason to believe that his struggle might come to an end. In February, he was

(left) This is one of several covers that Gauguin prepared for Noa Noa.

(right) Folio 63 from a manuscript of Noa Noa.

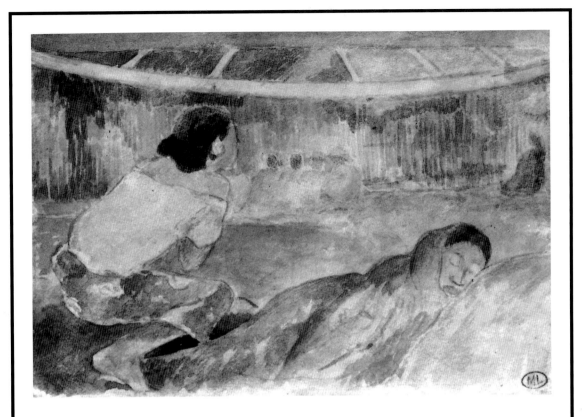

appointed editor-in-chief of *Les Guêpes*; it was a well-paid position that earned him respect in the community. And, far more important, in March he signed a contract with Ambroise Vollard, an enterprising and clever Parisian art dealer, who agreed to purchase a fixed number of canvases from Gauguin each year for a steady monthly sum. Through the paintings he managed to complete and send to Paris, his fame was growing, and his work was finally beginning to sell. He would, at last, be free to spend his time peacefully in Tahiti, painting without the concerns that had tormented him for so many years.

It was, however, too late. His imagination, he wrote Monfreid, was "beginning to grow cold in Tahiti." Once again, he needed a change, and he again made plans to move to the far more primitive Marquesas Islands. "I think that there, the altogether wild element, the complete solitude will give me a last burst of enthusiasm which will rejuvenate my imagination and lead to the fulfillment of my talent before I die," he wrote to Charles Morice.

Having paid off his debts, sold his house, and given up his career

as a journalist in Tahiti, Gauguin soon arrived in Atuona, the capital of Hivaoa, the most important and second largest of the islands, on September 16, 1901. In spite of its rugged beauty, the island was not paradise. Its population had been decimated by disease and further diminished by bloody tribal wars, and few foreigners chose to live there.

Gauguin, characteristically, paid no attention to this. Warmly greeted by the residents familiar with his writings for *Les*

No te aha oe riri (Why Are You Angry?). 1896 *This monumental canvas, painted after Gauguin's return to Tahiti, is based upon an earlier Tahitian painting. It is difficult to determine just who is angry, though it is probably the seated figure nearest to the standing figure.*

Guêpes, he soon bought a piece of land in the middle of the village and, with the help of two neighboring carpenters, set about building an extravagant two-story home. Splendidly and richly decorated, he called it "The House of Pleasure." For the painter's first months on the island, it was just that. Happy crowds of natives gathered there each evening, staring at the pictures that covered the walls of his studio, dancing, singing, and playing his guitar and mandolin.

By the middle of November, Gauguin settled down. Having found another *vahine,* Vaeoho, to keep him company and run his home, he gave fewer parties and spent more of his time exploring the island. January 1902 marked the beginning of a tremendously productive period of work. Experimenting more and more with the use of color, he painted still lifes, portraits, Biblical scenes, and mythological scenes with a renewed strength and vigor. By March he wrote Monfreid that soon he would arrange to have thirty-two new paintings sent to France—twelve to Monfreid and twenty to Vollard.

This burst of enthusiasm—as he himself had predicted—proved to be Gauguin's last. Soon, his health worsened, and by July he bought a horse and wagon because he had such difficulty walking. Unable to paint, he again became an angry spokesman for the French residents as well as for the natives; he refused to pay his own taxes and urged others to do the same. In the middle of August, Vaeoho, pregnant, went to her family's home to have her baby and never returned. Gauguin was alone. By September, wracked with pain and unable to sleep without the aid of morphine, he wrote Monfreid that he would travel to Paris for medical aid, after which he would settle in Spain. His friend advised him against it, urging him not to return to France for another few years. "You are a unique and legendary artist," he wrote. "You already belong to the history of art." And, he implied,

---

Primitive Tales. *1902*

In this mysterious, haunting late work, the figure of Gauguin's old friend Meyer de Haan looks over the two figures of Tahitian women—one of them in a Buddhalike pose.

his return to France might destroy that legend and jeopardize his position.

By the time he received this reply, Gauguin was a dying man. He was seldom able to paint, and, falling behind in his commitment to Vollard, he sent him paintings he had done some years earlier. Instead, he directed all of his energies into his writing. He wrote essays attacking his enemies, on and off the islands—the Catholic church, the state, French art critics, and the institution of marriage. And he kept a kind of diary, combined with a number of recollections, which he called *Avant et après (Before and After)*.

Gauguin soon put his words into action. He battled actively against the abuses of the colonial government and fought for the rights of the natives. After a while, government officials retaliated. On March 27, 1903, he was brought to court for libeling a policeman and was sentenced to three months in prison.

Too weak to appeal the sentence, before serving his time he closed himself in his house for a full week. At the end of it, he sent for one of his few good friends, the pastor Vernier, who, on May 8, found him in bed, writhing in pain. After the pastor left a few hours later, Tioka, a carpenter who was his nearest neighbor, found him inert, one leg hanging over the side of his bed. Fearing the worst, Tioka, following the traditional Marquesan custom, bit his head to determine whether he was alive. Gauguin remained motionless. He had died alone, as he had lived much of his life.

He was buried, with little ceremony, in the Catholic cemetery above Atuona the following day, but word of his death did not reach Paris until late August. Two months after that, the French public learned that Paul Gauguin was far more than a colorful, exotic legend. Along with the most important critics and artists of the

(left) In this self-portrait with glasses, painted in 1903, the year of his death, the artist, serious and somber, looks older than his fifty-four years.

(right) On Saturday, May 9, 1903, Gauguin was buried in a cemetery over-looking the village of Atuona. This tombstone marks his grave.

time, they crowded into the Ambroise Vollard gallery, where an exhibition of fifty paintings and twenty-seven drawings revealed him to be an immensely powerful and strikingly original artist.

Since that time, Gauguin's fame, which continually eluded him throughout his lifetime, has steadily grown. The recognition of his enormous talent has become universally recognized; hundreds of books and articles have been written about him, and his works hang in the world's greatest museums. His bold use of color and form has influenced scores of artists who followed him, among them Pablo Picasso and Henri Matisse. He will be remembered as an innovator, a courageous painter who dared to experiment, and whose experiments led to the creation of some of the world's best-loved works of art.

List of Illustrations